Date: 8/21/14

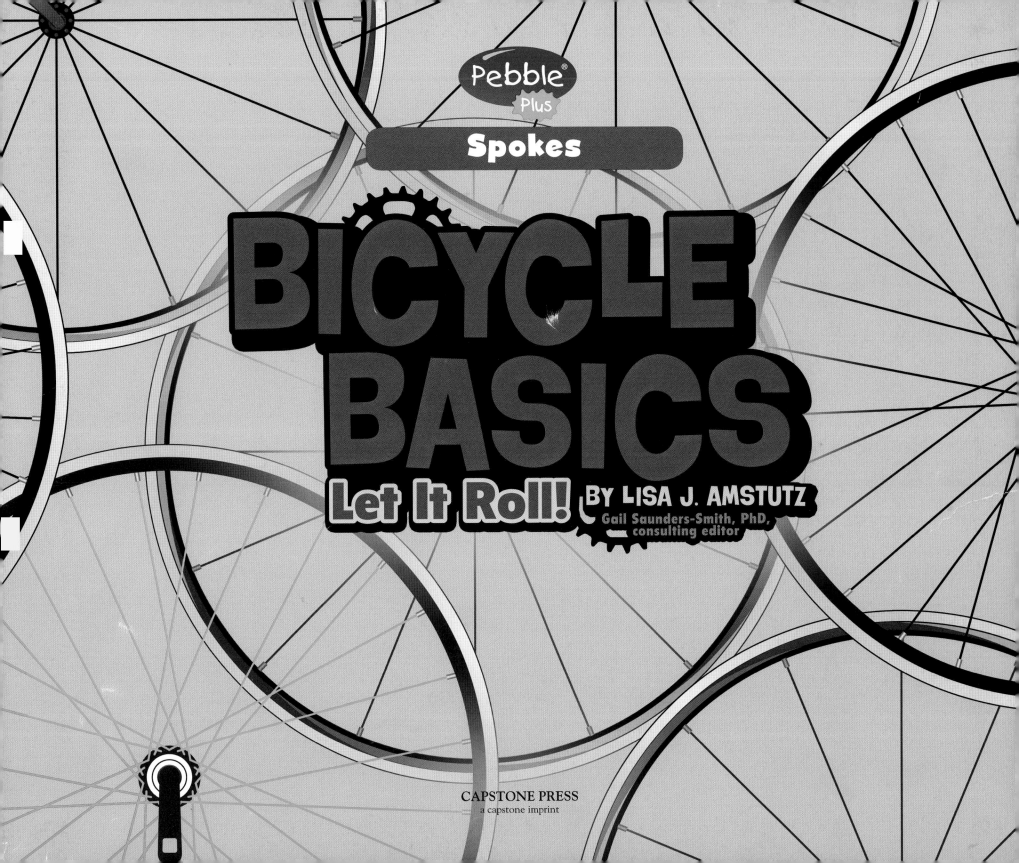

Pebble® Plus

Spokes

BICYCLE BASICS

Let It Roll!

BY LISA J. AMSTUTZ

Gail Saunders-Smith, PhD,
consulting editor

CAPSTONE PRESS
a capstone imprint

Pebble Plus is published by Capstone Press,
1710 Roe Crest Drive, North Mankato, Minnesota 56003.
www.capstonepub.com

Library of Congress Cataloging-in-Publication Data
Amstutz, Lisa J.
Bike basics: let it roll! / by Lisa J. Amstutz.
pages cm.—(Pebble plus. Spokes.)
Includes bibliographical references and index.
Summary: "Full-color photos and simple text provide an overview of bicycling"—Provided by publisher.
ISBN 978-1-4765-3964-5 (library binding)
ISBN 978-1-4765-6027-4 (ebook pdf)
1. Cycling—Juvenile literature. I. Title.
GV1043.5.A67 2014
796.6—dc23   2013031428

Editorial Credits
Jeni Wittrock, editor; Kyle Grenz, designer; Jennifer Walker, production specialist; Sarah Schuette, photo stylist;
Marcy Morin, photo scheduler

Photo Credits
Capstone Studio: Karon Dubke, cover; Corbis: Tom Stewart, 5, Dreamstime: Brad Calkins, 17; Newscom: World History
Archive, 13; Shutterstock: fotum, 15, Hodag Media, 11, homydesign, 7, Jean-Michel Girard, 20, Monkey Business Images, 19,
21; Wikimedia: Lokilech, 9

Design Elements
Shutterstock: filip robert, Kalmatsuy Tatyana

Note to Parents and Teachers

The Spokes set supports national standards related to physical education and recreation. This
book presents and illustrates basic knowledge of bicycling. The images support early readers in
understanding the text. The repetition of words and phrases helps early readers learn new words.
This book also introduces early readers to subject-specific vocabulary words, which are defined in
the Glossary section. Early readers may need assistance to read some words and to use the Table of
Contents, Glossary, Read More, Internet Sites, and Index sections of the book.

Printed in the United States of America in North Mankato, Minnesota.
092013   007775CGS14

Table of Contents

Let's Ride!

Have somewhere to go? Ride a bike! Bikes do not pollute the air like cars do. Biking is good exercise too. Most of all, biking is fun.

Bikes come in many shapes and sizes. Some bikes are for racing. Others are for jumps and tricks. But bikes weren't always easy to use.

The History of Bicycles

The first bicycle was invented in 1817. It had two wheels but no pedals. The word bicycle means "two-wheel."

Pedals were added in 1839. Early pedal bikes were hard to ride. Some were very tall. If riders fell off, they often got hurt.

In 1885 J. K. Starley built the safety bicycle. A chain turned its wheels. Today's bikes are faster and lighter. But they work the same way.

13

How a Bike Works

To ride a bike, push the pedals with your feet.

The pedals turn a large cog and chain. The chain turns the back wheel. Off you go!

pedal

cog

chain

A bike's rubber tires wrap

around metal rims.

Tires make rides less bumpy.

The hubs and spokes give

bike wheels strength.

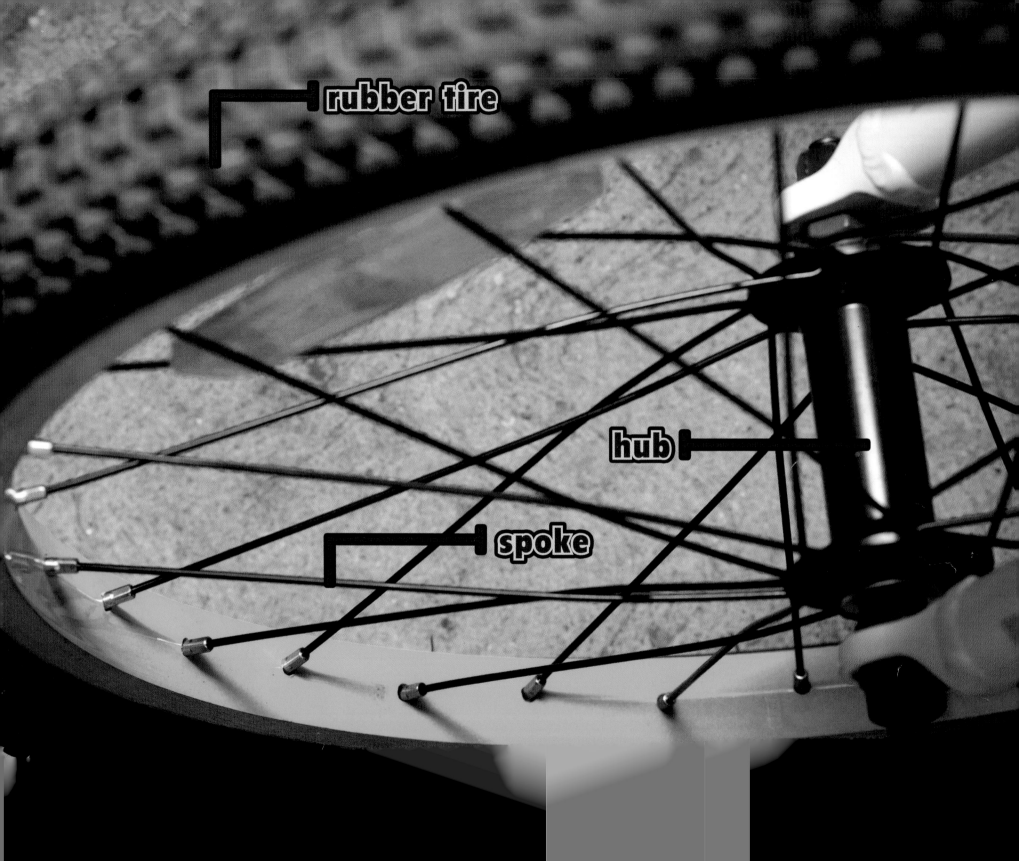

rubber tire

hub

spoke

To steer a bike, turn
the handlebars. Use the
brakes to stop or slow down.
Done biking? When you park,
put down the kickstand.

Bike Safety

It is important to ride safely. Follow traffic rules. When you want to stop or turn, use hand signals. Always wear a helmet, and have fun!

hand signals

left   right   stop

Glossary

brake—a tool that slows down or stops a bike

cog—a toothed wheel

handlebar—the part of a bicycle that the rider holds on to and uses to steer

hand signal—a special sign to show others that you plan to stop or turn

hub—the center part of a wheel

invent—think up and make something new

kickstand—a piece of metal that sticks out to balance a parked bicycle

pedal—a lever on a bicycle that riders push with their feet

pollute—to make something dirty or unsafe

rim—the metal circle inside the tire

spoke—a bar that goes out from the center of the wheel to support the rim

strength—the quality of being strong

tire—a ring of rubber on the outside of a wheel; a tube of air fits inside

traffic—vehicles that are moving on a road

Read More

Hamilton, Robert M. *On a Bike.* Going Places. New York: Gareth Stevens Pub., 2012.

Mara, Wil. *What Should I Do? On My Bike.* Community Connections. Ann Arbor, Mich.: Cherry Lake Pub., 2012.

Maurer, Tracy Nelson. *Bicycle Riding.* Sports for Sprouts. Vero Beach, Fla.: Rourke Pub., 2011.

Internet Sites

FactHound offers a safe, fun way to find Internet sites related to this book. All of the sites on FactHound have been researched by our staff.

Here's all you do:

Visit *www.facthound.com*

Type in this code: 9781476539645

 **Super-cool stuff!** Check out projects, games and lots more at **www.capstonekids.com**

Index

Word Count: 219
Grade: 1
Early-Intervention Level: 14